POP PERFORMANCE PIECES

Violin & Piano

ALL OF ME JOHN LEGEND 2

BRIDGE OVER TROUBLED WATER SIMON & GARFUNKEL 8

CLOCKS COLDPLAY 16

DON'T STOP BELIEVIN' JOURNEY 22

FIREWORK KATY PERRY 29

MAD WORLD MICHAEL ANDREWS FEAT. GARY JULES 34

A THOUSAND MILES VANESSA CARLTON 42

A THOUSAND YEARS CHRISTINA PERRI 37

WHEN WE WERE YOUNG ADELE 52

YOUR SONG ELTON JOHN 48

Published by
Chester Music
part of The Music Sales Group
14-15 Berners Street,
London W1T 3LJ, UK.

Exclusive Distributors:
Music Sales Limited
Distribution Centre, Newmarket Road,
Bury St Edmunds, Suffolk IP33 3YB, UK.
Music Sales Pty Limited
Level 4, Lisgar House,
30-32 Carrington Street,
Sydney, NSW 2000 Australia.

Order No. CH85041
ISBN 978-1-78558-332-2

Piano scores are transposed.
Chord symbols at concert pitch.

Violin consultant: Mary Kelly.
Piano consultant: Lisa Cox.
Compiled and edited by Naomi Cook.
Music formatted by Sarah Lofthouse, SEL Music Art Ltd.

Photographs courtesy of Ruth Keating,
assisted by Lisa Cox and James Welland.
Special thanks to the pupils at St Benedict's School, Ealing
and their Director of Music Christopher Eastwood for taking
part in the photo shoot.

Printed in the EU.

Your Guarantee of Quality
As publishers, we strive to produce every book to
the highest commercial standards. This book has
been carefully designed to minimise awkward
page turns and to make playing from it a real
pleasure. Particular care has been given to
specifying acid-free, neutral-sized paper made
from pulps which have not been elemental chlorine
bleached. This pulp is from farmed sustainable
forests and was produced with special regard for
the environment. Throughout, the printing and
binding have been planned to ensure a sturdy,
attractive publication which should give years
of enjoyment. If your copy fails to meet our high
standards, please inform us and we will gladly
replace it.

www.musicsales.com

CHESTER MUSIC
part of The Music Sales Group
London / New York / Paris / Sydney / Copenhagen / Berlin / Madrid / Hong Kong / Tokyo

ALL OF ME

Words & Music by John Legend & Tobias Gad

Hints & Tips: Make sure you use the dynamics to help build interest in the piece, being careful not to overpower the melody. There are many held notes throughout — resist the urge to rely on the pedal to sustain the notes rather than holding them for their full value. Practise without the pedal first!

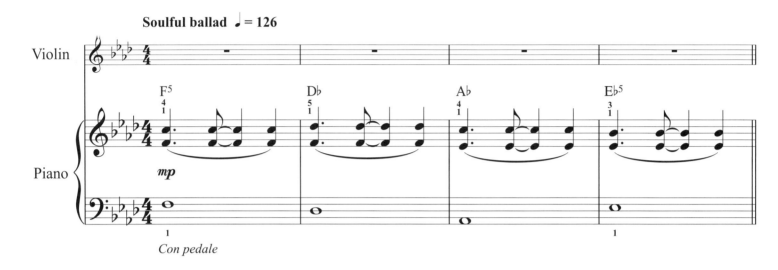

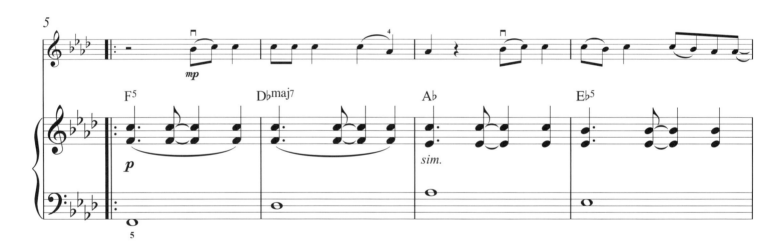

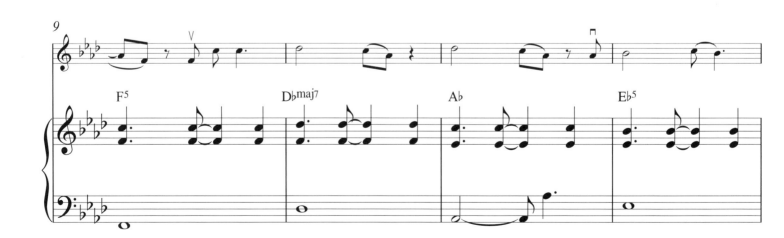

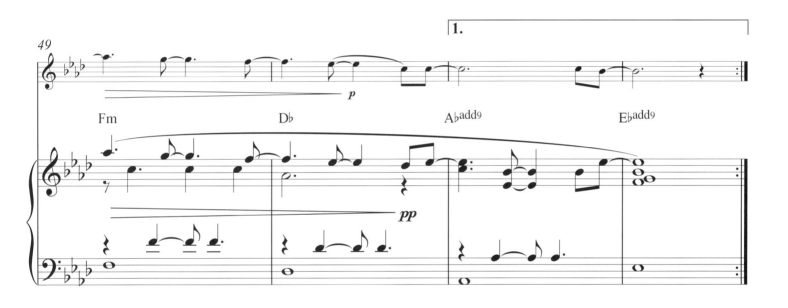

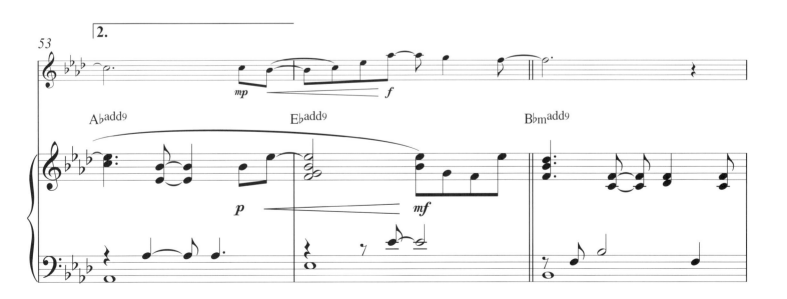

BRIDGE OVER TROUBLED WATER

Words & Music by Paul Simon

Hints & Tips: There are lots of block chords in this piece: make sure you use the correct fingers
in anticipation of the next chord position. Watch out for the accidentals too!

CLOCKS

Words & Music by Guy Berryman, Jonathan Buckland,
William Champion & Christopher Martin

Hints & Tips: Keep the left hand crisp and on the beat and pay attention to keeping a steady pulse. From bar 53 there is a repeated quaver pattern in the right hand played with the 5th finger — make sure the quavers are even as this finger can get tired quite quickly.

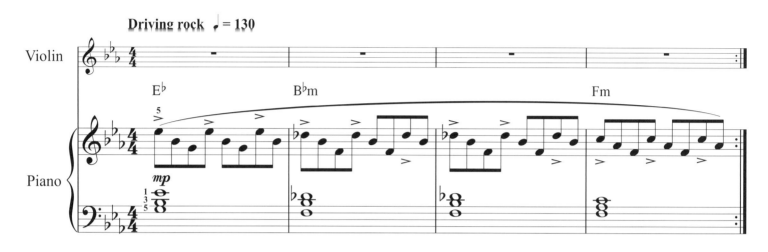

DON'T STOP BELIEVIN'

Words & Music by Steve Perry, Neal Schon & Jonathan Cain

Hints & Tips: Bring out the famous bass line in the left hand and watch out for the off-beat rhythms — make sure you count carefully to ensure every note falls in the right place. Work with the soloist to ensure you play your shared rhythms exactly together in the chorus (e.g. bars 41 and 42).

Rock ♩ = 116

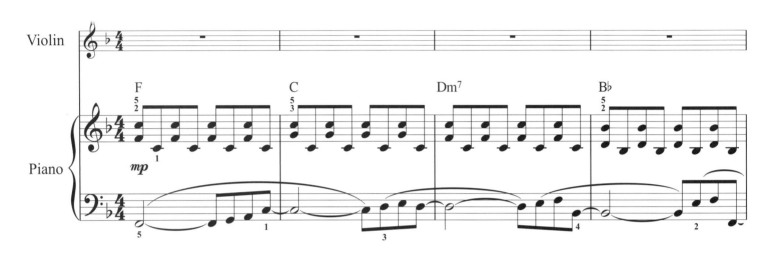

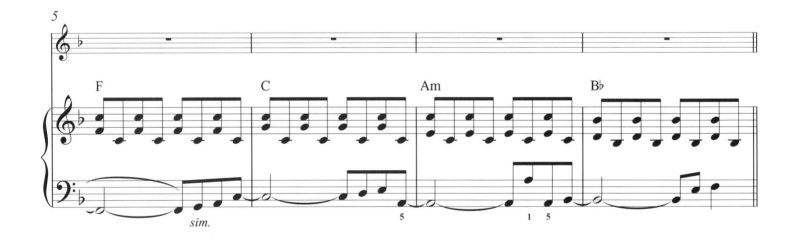

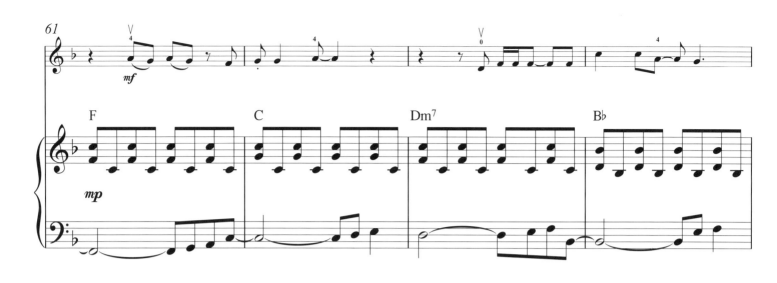

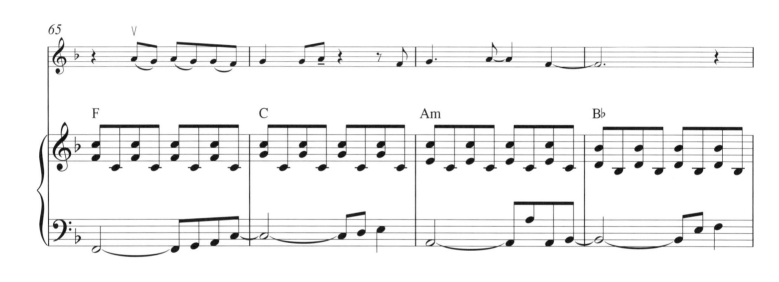

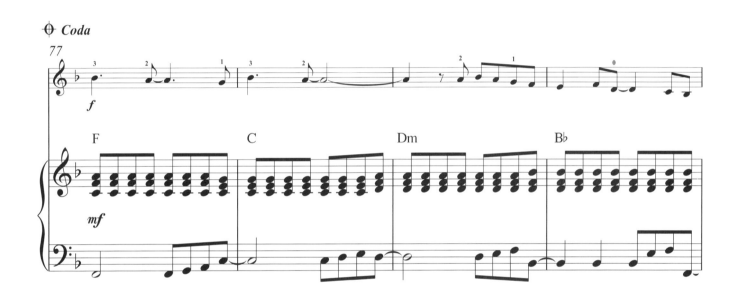

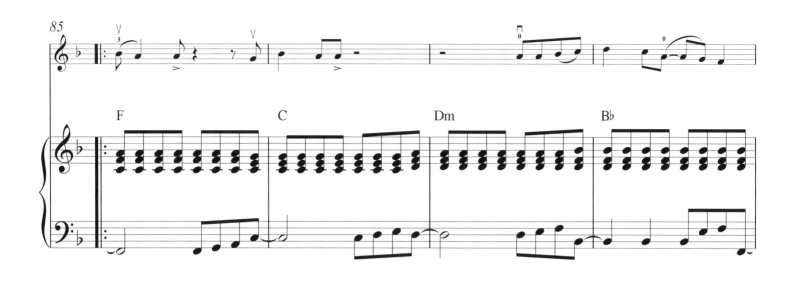

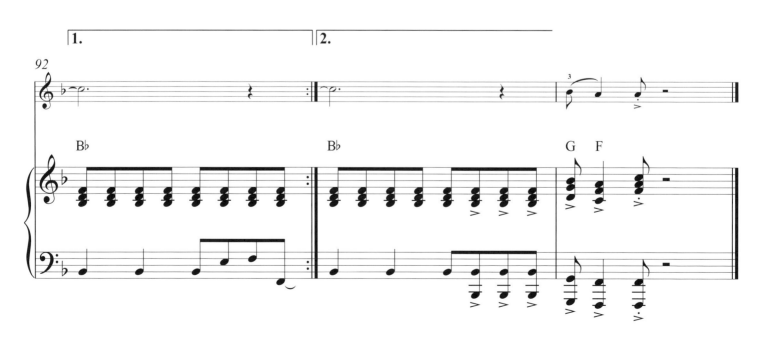

POP PERFORMANCE
PIECES

Published by
Chester Music
part of The Music Sales Group
14-15 Berners Street,
London W1T 3LJ, UK.

Exclusive Distributors:
Music Sales Limited
Distribution Centre, Newmarket Road,
Bury St Edmunds, Suffolk IP33 3YB, UK.
Music Sales Pty Limited
Level 4, Lisgar House,
30-32 Carrington Street,
Sydney, NSW 2000 Australia.

Order No. CH85041
ISBN 978-1-78558-332-2

This book © Copyright 2016 Wise Publications,
a division of Music Sales Limited.

Piano scores are transposed.
Chord symbols at concert pitch.

Violin consultant: Mary Kelly.
Piano consultant: Lisa Cox.
Compiled and edited by Naomi Cook.
Music formatted by Sarah Lofthouse, SEL Music Art Ltd.

Photographs courtesy of Ruth Keating,
assisted by Lisa Cox and James Welland.
Special thanks to the pupils at St Benedict's School, Ealing
and their Director of Music Christopher Eastwood for taking
part in the photo shoot.

Printed in the EU.

Your Guarantee of Quality
As publishers, we strive to produce every book to
the highest commercial standards. This book has
been carefully designed to minimise awkward
page turns and to make playing from it a real
pleasure. Particular care has been given to
specifying acid-free, neutral-sized paper made
from pulps which have not been elemental chlorine
bleached. This pulp is from farmed sustainable
forests and was produced with special regard for
the environment. Throughout, the printing and
binding have been planned to ensure a sturdy,
attractive publication which should give years
of enjoyment.If your copy fails to meet our high
standards, please inform us and we will gladly
replace it.

www.musicsales.com

POP PERFORMANCE PIECES

Violin Part

ALL OF ME JOHN LEGEND 4

BRIDGE OVER TROUBLED WATER SIMON & GARFUNKEL 6

CLOCKS COLDPLAY 8

DON'T STOP BELIEVIN' JOURNEY 10

FIREWORK KATY PERRY 12

MAD WORLD MICHAEL ANDREWS FEAT. GARY JULES 22

A THOUSAND MILES VANESSA CARLTON 14

A THOUSAND YEARS CHRISTINA PERRI 16

WHEN WE WERE YOUNG ADELE 18

YOUR SONG ELTON JOHN 20

CHESTER MUSIC
part of The Music Sales Group
London / New York / Paris / Sydney / Copenhagen / Berlin / Madrid / Hong Kong / Tokyo

ALL OF ME

Words & Music by John Legend & Tobias Gad

Hints & Tips: Before you start, practise your two-octave A♭ major scale (slurred bows), paying special attention to the transition between the A and E strings. Watch out for the transition to 3rd position at bar 19!

BRIDGE OVER TROUBLED WATER

Words & Music by Paul Simon

Hints & Tips: This piece is great for practising 2nd position. Play the F major scale (one octave) in 2nd position as a warm-up. Practise glissandi from F (D string) to F (3rd position A string).

CLOCKS

Words & Music by Guy Berryman, Jonathan Buckland,
William Champion & Christopher Martin

Hints & Tips: This piece will make you an expert at E♭ major and A♭ major scales! Remember that every
4th finger in the piece will be low. Some 3rd fingers will be low too — which ones?

9

DON'T STOP BELIEVIN'

Words & Music by Steve Perry, Neal Schon & Jonathan Cain

Hints & Tips: Use your 4th finger instead of an open string wherever indicated to build up the strength in your finger. Practise shifting from 1st to 3rd position (bars 35–36).

FIREWORK

Words & Music by Tor Erik Hermansen, Katy Perry,
Mikkel S. Eriksen, Sandy Wilhelm & Ester Dean

Hints & Tips: Make the most of the dynamics in this piece, especially the build up from bars 20 to 28.
Watch out for the 4th finger extension in bar 74!

A THOUSAND MILES

Words & Music by Vanessa Carlton

Hints & Tips: Long notes can sneak up on you — try not to get stuck in one part of your bow! Sometimes it's easier to use an open string than a 4th finger, but sometimes a 4th finger sounds better. Can you figure out why?

A THOUSAND YEARS

Words & Music by David Hodges & Christina Perri

Hints & Tips: Prepare for this piece by practising your two-octave B♭ major scale, paying special attention to the transition from E♭ to F (as in bar 7). Remember to save your bow in bar 22 so you can keep going through bar 23!

17

WHEN WE WERE YOUNG

Words & Music by Adele Adkins & Tobias Jesso

Hints & Tips: This piece will help you become very good at quickly switching between 1st and 3rd position.
Bars 43 and 44 are great for practising syncopated rhythms.

19

YOUR SONG

Words & Music by Elton John & Bernie Taupin

Hints & Tips: There are lots of 'Scotch snap' (semiquaver-dotted quaver) rhythms — make sure you're ready for them! It may help to clap through the piece first.

MAD WORLD

Words & Music by Roland Orzabal

Hints & Tips: You can use open strings instead of 4th fingers to begin with. Try adding in more 4th fingers as you become familiar with the tune, to build up the strength in your finger.

123456789

Chester Music
part of The Music Sales Group
CH85041
www.musicsales.com

FIREWORK

Words & Music by Tor Erik Hermansen, Katy Perry,
Mikkel S. Eriksen, Sandy Wilhelm & Ester Dean

Hints & Tips: Make sure the driving quaver pattern in crisp and clear throughout.
Watch out for the change to off-beat rhythms at bar 45!

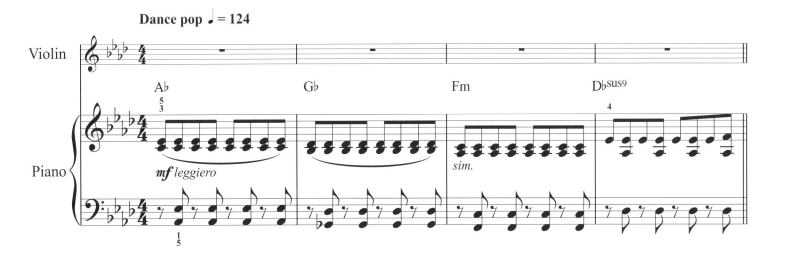

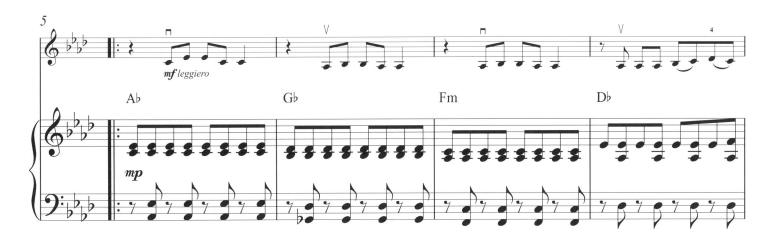

MAD WORLD

Words & Music by Roland Orzabal

Hints & Tips: Make sure the dynamic of the broken chord pattern stays the same when it switches to the right hand in bar 5. Bring out the lovely counter-melody in the right hand at bar 29. The rhythms are less predictable in the right hand from bar 22 — count carefully!

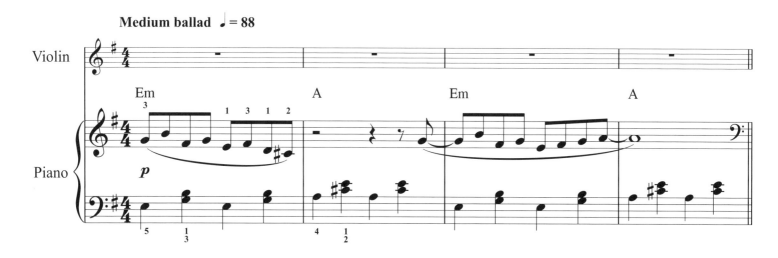

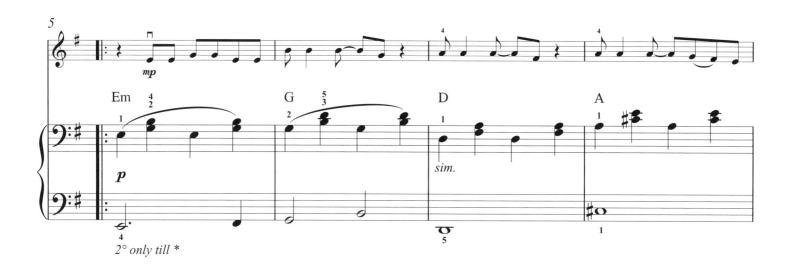

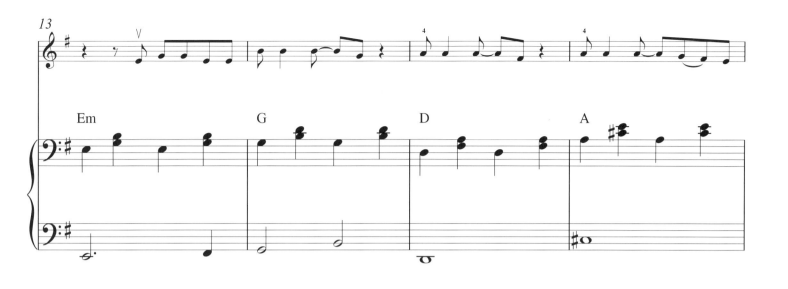

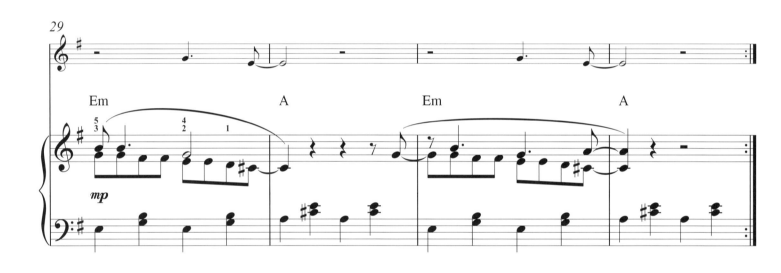

A THOUSAND YEARS

Words & Music by David Hodges & Christina Perri

Hints & Tips: There is a broad range of dynamics in this piece; make sure you make the most of these contrasts. Practise playing the right hand duplets in bar 11 against the quavers in the left hand until you are secure with the rhythms. Use the pedal to sustain the block chords in the right hand from bar 23.

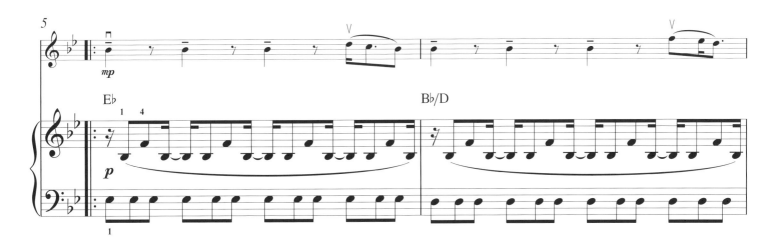

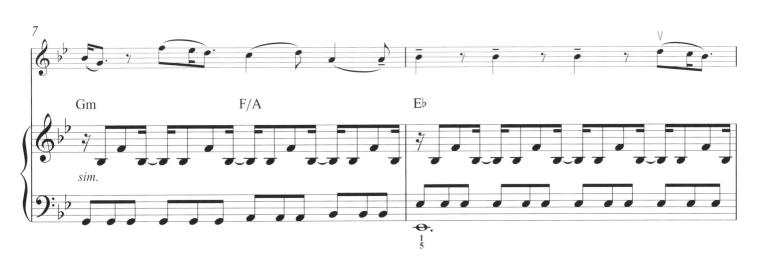

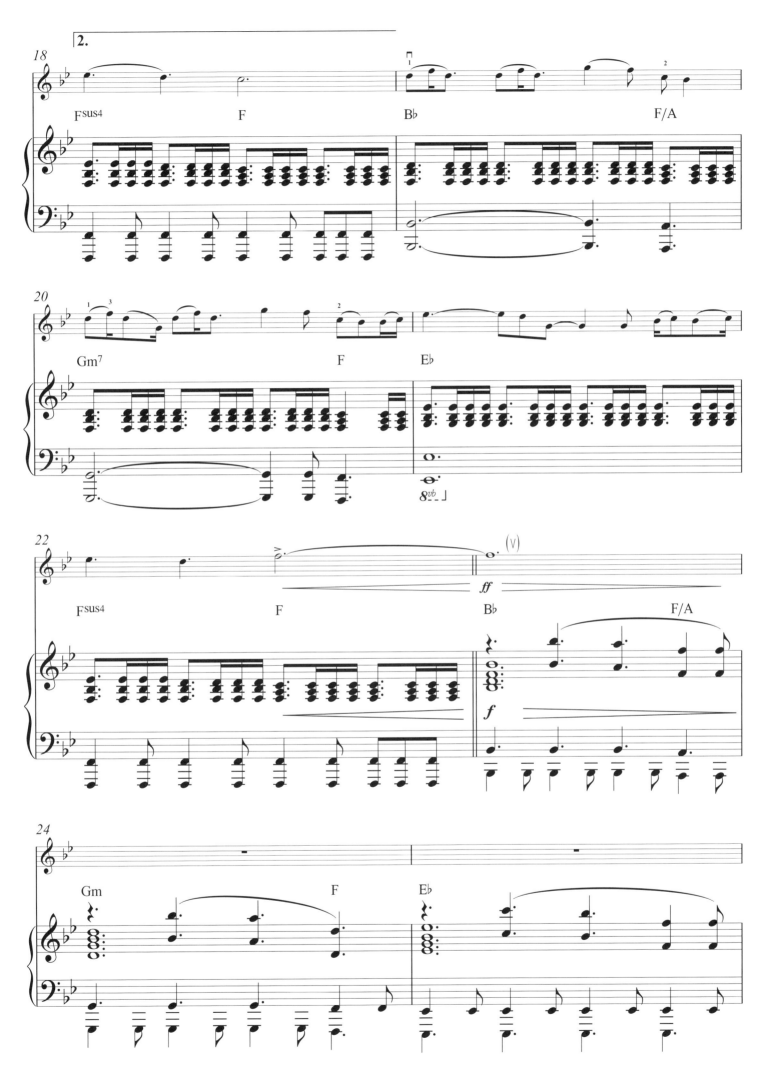

40

A THOUSAND MILES

Words & Music by Vanessa Carlton

Hints & Tips: This piece features a brilliant piano part! Remember to keep the semiquaver patterns crisp and even. There is a lot of movement in both hands so make sure you're ready for the octave jumps. Practise the call-and-response passages with the soloist (from bars 14 and 40), ensuring you keep to a steady tempo.

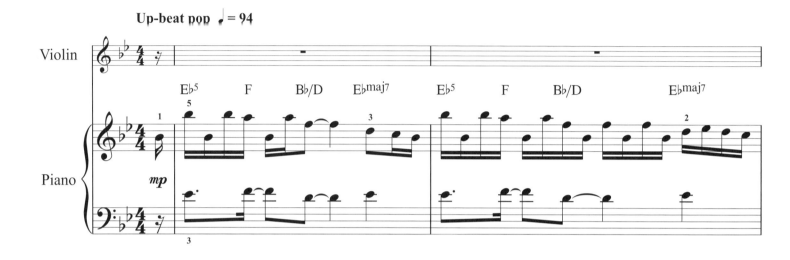

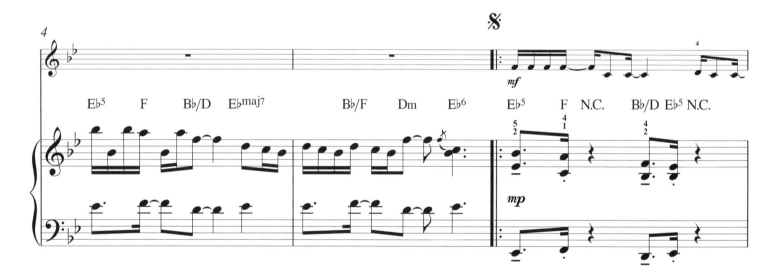

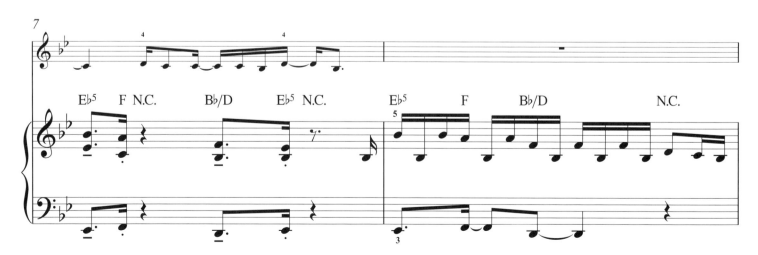

45

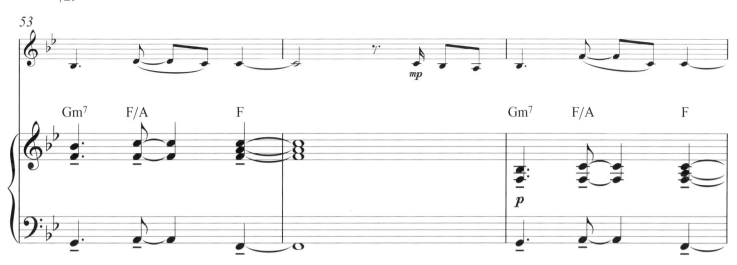

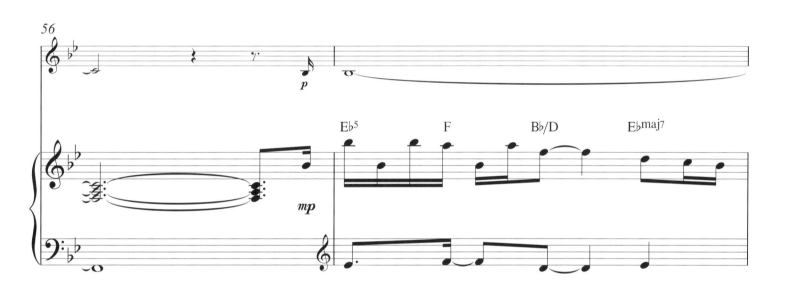

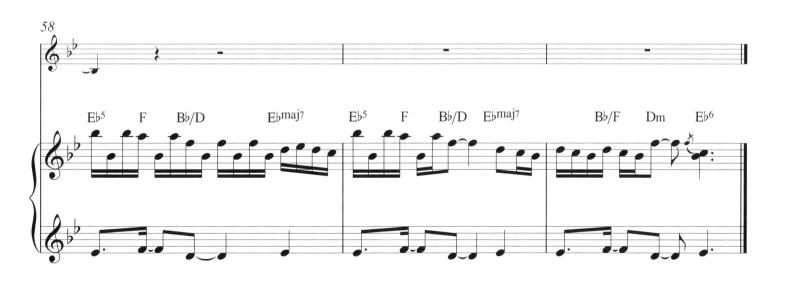

YOUR SONG

Words & Music by Elton John & Bernie Taupin

Hints & Tips: This piano part is quite busy so it's important to be sensitive to the soloist, being careful not to overpower them. Make sure you lift the pedal for every change in harmony so the sound doesn't become muddy. Some of the chords involve big stretches: play all the notes together first to get used to the shapes.

WHEN WE WERE YOUNG

Words & Music by Adele Adkins & Tobias Jesso

Hints & Tips: Work on getting the chord changes as smooth as possible and make sure you feel a steady pulse so you're not tempted to rush the held notes at the start of the piece. If the double octaves in the left hand are too big a stretch, just play the bottom note. Watch out for the big jump in both hands at bar 47!

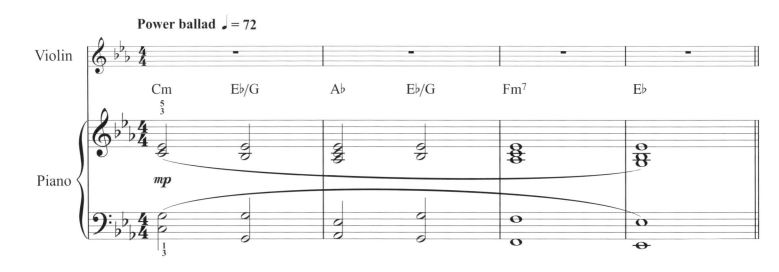

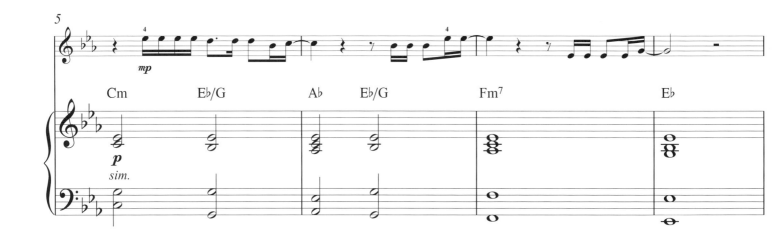

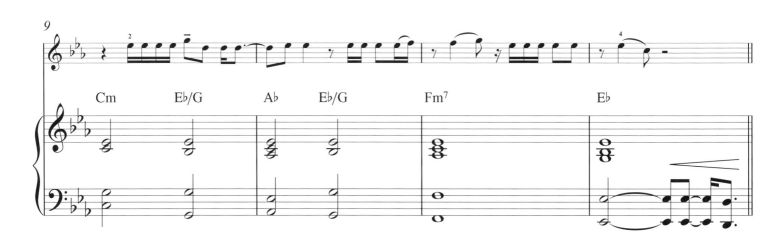